Food COLORS

From Blueberries to Beets

by Joyce Markovics

Consultant: Kimberly Brenneman, PhD
National Institute for Early Education Research, Rutgers University
New Brunswick, New Jersey

BEARPORT PUBLISHING

New York, New York

Credits

TOC, © Pablo Hidalgo, Alexander Sayenko, BLACKDAY/Shutterstock; 4–5, © Shutterstock; 6–7, © Creative Imagery/the food passionates/Corbis; 8, © Aksenova Natalya, Boule/Shutterstock; 9, © Dr.Margorius/Shutterstock; 10, © Switch, age fotostock/Alamy; 11, © D. Hurst/Alamy; 12, © Shutterstock; 13, © Snvv/Shutterstock; 14–15, © Julian Rovagnati/Shutterstock; 16–17, © SafakOguz/Thinkstock; 18, © Ruta Saulyte-Laurinaviciene/Shutterstock; 19, © Tim Gainey/Alamy; 20–21, © Elena Schweitzer/Shutterstock; 22, © s_oleg/Shutterstock; 23TL, © Imagemore/Superstock; 23TR, © Rosenfeld/Maritius/Superstock; 23BL, © MC_PP/Shutterstock; 23BR, © Javier Rosano/Shutterstock; 24, © Valentina Razumova, oriori/Shutterstock.

Publisher: Kenn Goin
Senior Editor: Joyce Tavolacci
Creative Director: Spencer Brinker
Design: Debrah Kaiser
Photo Researcher: Picture Perfect Professionals, LLC

Library of Congress Cataloging-in-Publication Data

Markovics, Joyce L., author.
  Food colors : from blueberries to beets / by Joyce Markovics.
      pages cm.—(Colors tell a story)
  Includes bibliographical references and index.
  ISBN-13: 978-1-62724-324-7 (library binding)
  ISBN-10: 1-62724-324-0 (library binding)
  1. Colors—Juvenile literature. 2. Food—Juvenile literature. I. Title.
QC495.5.M3677 2015
535.6—dc23
                                        2014009030

For more information, write to Bearport Publishing Company, Inc., 45 West 21st Street, Suite 3B, New York, New York 10010. Printed in the United States of America.

10 9 8 7 6 5 4 3 2 1

Contents

Food Colors

Colors tell a delicious story about food.

They let us know when food is ready to eat.

Get ready for a colorful feast!

Blueberries **ripen** on a bush.

They are pale green at first.

Then they become dark blue and delicious!

7

Crack an egg into a hot pan.

The egg is clear with a bright-yellow center.

As it cooks, the clear part changes to white.

9

Take a spoonful of
dark-brown **cocoa**.

Stir it into hot white milk.

When the milk is
light brown, the hot
chocolate is ready
to drink!

11

Apples come in many colors.

Some are golden yellow,
deep red, or bright green.

Each kind has a different, yummy flavor.

Bananas start
out green.

As they ripen, their **peels**
turn yellow.

Eat them up fast
before too many
dark-brown spots
appear!

Place some dough into the oven.

At first, the dough is soft and light tan.

After it's baked, the dough is crispy and golden brown.

Above the ground is a leafy green top.

Tug and pull the leaves.

Out pops a beet.

If the beet is dark red, it's ready to eat!

Eat a **rainbow** of colorful fruits and veggies!

They will make you strong and healthy.

They taste great, too.

Explore More: Make Food Paints

Many foods have bright, beautiful colors. You can use some of them to make paints—and then create a picture!

How to Make Food Paints:

1. Put a small amount of each colorful food in a separate section of the muffin tin. Mash up foods such as beets and blueberries. Be careful not to stain your clothing.

2. Place a few drops of water in each section of the tin.

3. Use a spoon to mix the food and water so it makes paint.

4. Create a picture using the paintbrushes and food paints. Be sure to use a different brush for each color.

5. When you are finished, show your painting to friends and family. Point out the different colors and explain what foods they came from.

You Will Need:

- Colorful foods, such as beets, blueberries, dry mustard, paprika, and cocoa powder
- Muffin tin
- Water
- Spoon
- Paintbrushes
- Paper

Glossary

cocoa (KOH-koh) a brown powder made by grinding up seeds from the cacao tree; used to make chocolate

peels (PEELZ) the outer skins of fruit

rainbow (RAYN-*boh*) an arch of different colors that sometimes appears in the sky after it rains; a variety of colors

ripen (RIPE-uhn) to become ready to eat

Index

Read More

Freymann, Saxton. *Food for Thought.* New York: Arthur A. Levine Books (2005).

Nordine, Ken. *Colors.* San Diego: Harcourt (2000).

Learn More Online

To learn more about food colors, visit
www.bearportpublishing.com/ColorsTellaStory

About the Author

Joyce Markovics and her husband, Adam, live along the Hudson River in Tarrytown, New York.

24